# Psych Ward Chronicles

# True George

# <u>Introduction</u>

Each story told is a chronicle of events that took place at a well-known Psychiatric center in New York City. The events were witnessed and documented by True_George who was serving as an Intern in the Psychiatric Center to complete the education requirements of the Long Island University Mental Health Counselor program.

The account was originally a student journal documenting activities and experience that was presented to the internship class during the classroom portion of the internship phase of the program. Events and experience were discussed to help with understanding and improving the approach to therapy and interacting with the mentally ill patients.

After graduating the work was re-written and featured on the blog True_George (www.truegeorge.com) under the category "Psych Ward Chronicles."

The patient's names have been changed to protect their identities. The Hospital is just referred to as the Psych Ward

True George

# <u>Contents</u>

# <u>State Sponsored</u>

If someone who has never been in a Psych Ward were to make a visit, they would get the impression that there is nothing going on except for the patients walking around like zombies and that staff is uncaring and look the other way leaving patients to fend for themselves. But the reality of the matter is that there is some type of organization. Patients are not left to fend for themselves; after all, mentally ill people are dependents and cannot truly function without support whether that support is direct or indirect.

The programmed scheduled time remains the same seven days a week. In the morning after the patients do their personal hygiene they are taken to breakfast. After they return around nine O'clock the medication is administered. During the administering of the medication it is the most stressful part of the day for most patients. After the administering of the medication is over it seems the patients are not in a sociable mood.

During the week those who have appointments outside the Psych Ward are escorted by one of the Psych Ward staff to their respective appointment. They get chauffeured to and from the appointment in a van; complements of the State's Office of Mental Health (OMH). Other patients attend their various therapy programs within the Psych Ward's grounds. While those that were just admitted or are too unstable do not leave the ward.

The programs and the content which the therapists use is all dictated by the State. The material that the therapist use comes directly from a state published work book. A manual called the "Wellness Self-Management Treatment." The manual covers all the subjects that the Psych Ward uses to provide the group treatment programs that the facility runs every day. In essence whatever focus group the patients attend is based on the information and outline that is in the manual. Likewise, for individual therapy it is all covered in manuals that are state published.

On the weekend most of the patients remain in their room. There are only a few of them in the common day area on Saturday, and on Sunday the day area is deserted. It is not a requirement that the patients engage in any activity on the weekends.

After lunch is when most of the patients leave their room and mingle around in the common day area. This is when the Interns get patients involved in a recreation game.

Without any structure or help from staff getting patients involved in a game creates the opportunity to gain rapport with the patient and to get any type of information.

It is the kind of information that is not written in the patient's charts. Patients will tell who is having conflict with whom; whether it's patient on patient, staff on patient or staff on staff.

The patients observe how the staff behaves and they know how much they can get away with doing things against the Psych wards rules depending on which staff member is on duty.

Everything in the Psych Ward is state sponsored. The State owns the buildings, pays the staff, dictates how therapy is conducted, dictates the staff's code of conduct, dictates the conditions of patient admittance and discharge, dictates when visitors are allowed to come and what they can bring, the state even dictates the entire schedule.

The saying is if gov't has a hand in things, they always mess it up. It is a wonder that the state does not truly provide for the needs of the mentally ill. The state-run programs just scratch the surface and once there is a measure of stability the mentally ill person is cut lose without any type of support from the state for after care. 9 out of 10 times the mentally ill person is back in the Psych Ward at some point.

# <u>Side Effects</u>

This week the usually sleepy Psych Ward was lively. Patients that are usually quiet and stay in their rooms were roaming around. One of patients that stood out was Lydia. Her behavior makes staff and her fellow patients laugh. Yet her behavior also shows that she has a lot of unresolved mental issues. It is ironic because Dora who is one of the most unpredictable patients and who is usually the one who is involved in some sort of commotion was quiet.

Another patient that that stood out was Anna. She is the type of patient whose degree of awareness varies. One week she has some awareness and another week she has no type of awareness. But this week Anna was cognitively stable and was very aware. Anna explained to Intern Joseph that the new Doctor took her off Lithium. She said the Lithium side effects were very unpleasant.

When she took the Lithium, she had no type of awareness, she didn't know where she was, and on top of that she lost her memory.

She forgot how to write and she lost the ability to speak. Anna said that that she wanted to speak and that she knew what she wanted to say but the words would not come out. Sometimes she would get a couple of words out, but the words would be in Polish her native language and since no one spoke Polish nobody understood what she was saying.

Along with the lost abilities she was also having hallucinations. All she saw were mice. The mice were walking around the Psych Ward and in the light fixtures. Also because of her lost abilities to write and speak English she could not communicate with the treatment team to tell them what she was experiencing.

When a new Doctor was assigned to the Psych Ward, he looked at Anna's prescription and perhaps observed her behavior and recognized that she was experiencing unpleasant side effects from the lithium. The new Doctor immediately changed her prescription and replaced the lithium with another medication.

Chris also described how he felt cognitively; he cannot recall anything that took place in his life for a period of six months. Everything is totally blank. He doesn't even recall how or when he was admitted to the Psych Ward. All he remembers was that he was in the street then the next thing he remembers is being in the Psych Ward hanging up his clothes. The staff told him that he has been in the Psych Ward for the last six months.

The effects of the medication are perhaps one of the scariest parts of being a patient in the Psych Ward. In Anna's case, she was lucky that the newly assigned Doctor recognized that she was in trouble. The old Doctor, the treatment team and the staff who have daily contact with Anna failed to detect or recognize the effects of the medication. If the new Doctor was part of the regular routine, he probably would not have caught the drug's side effects either.

It is sad to think that once he gets acclimated to the Psych Ward's routine then the patients will feel the effects, and the effects won't be good for them.

This is not a good thing because if the treatment team and staff missed that one day a patient could perform basic spoken or written communication and the next day cannot communicate and speak a language they have not spoken since being admitted; which all took place after a change in medication. They need to be retrained. Perhaps no one cared, either way it was negligence, and gets you to think that there may be other patients in the Psych Ward who are experiencing negative side effects of their medication and it is being neglected.

In Chris's case the black out of memories for the past six months could have been the effects of self-medication.

Sometimes mentally ill people tend to take substances in order to feel better and relax. Marijuana is a common un-prescribed drug of choice, but street life is hard. The type of marijuana sold at a cheap rate is an inferior product. Either the weed is processed in a microwave or it is a synthetic imitation of marijuana; like K-2 or other brands.

Even when people with no mental illness smoke the synthetic imitation marijuana, they experience side effects that will compromise thinking and cognitive abilities.

The side effects are worse and magnified if a person with mental illness smoke those same inferior brands of marijuana. It is obvious that Chris was self-medicating and his symptoms suggested that he was smoking the inferior synthetic marijuana products. It has robbed him the memory of six months of his life.

# <u>Liaisons</u>

In the Psychiatric ward it is not like the patients are under watch 24/7 even though they are supposed to be. Unless the staff take a particular interest and take control of the ward then the patients have the run of the place. In New York State, the psychiatric institutions are Male and Female integrated.

Kevin is spending a considerable amount of time speaking to Pam. Staff need to pay attention to this because Kevin has a habit of soliciting the female patients for sex. He is probably taking advantage of Pam.

Being aware of this the Intern Joseph gestured to Kevin to come and play some cards in a game that the Intern organized. Kevin who is always a participant in the card games declined to participate.

Perhaps Mike probably has some insight into the unspoken actions that the patients engage in. The therapist casually mentioned to Mike, "I see that Kevin is trying to get know Pam." Mike responded "Pam is game, and Kevin should have fucked her already."

Mike also said" During the week Pam comes to my room and gives me pussy." Mike said that his roommate Dave occasionally walks in on him and Pam while they are having sex. When he does Pam sucks and has sex with both of them. How could this be?

How was Pam able to go into Mike's room when the staff could see everything from the desk?

Mike explained that when Marcus the aide on the night shift is on duty, he doesn't care what goes on between patients. He is sure that Marcus sees when Pam enters his room or sometimes, they enter the room together.

Instead of saying something, he turns the other way. Mike also said that since he arrived to the unit, he has been having sex with Ann-Marie. He also added that Dawn has been sucking dicks in exchange for cigarettes. One patient in particular Richard (youngest male patient) has been getting more head from Dawn than anyone else. This is because he has an abundance of contraband cigarettes and gets head from Dawn each time, she wants one.

It is was hard to believe that so much sexual activity is going on between patients who are there because of some type of psychiatric issue. All of it going on under the nose of the staff.

Yet, Mike's chart confirms that he has a history of being caught engaging in sexual activities at other psychiatry institutions during his years in the system. It is a wonder that Mike has enough trust in the Therapist to speak so freely about his activities in the unit. Or he just doesn't give a dam.

Mike has been in and out of Psychiatric Institutions since his childhood. It was unfortunate that Mike was born addicted to crack and his Psychiatric issues developed early in life.

In his stay at the last Psychiatric Institution he was arrested because a Nurse reported that he groped her breast and rubbed his genitals on her. Mike had to spend a couple of months in Prison because of it. He came directly to the unit when he was released from Riker's Island.

Pam is from the Ultra-Orthodox Jewish community. At one point she was married, it ended up in divorce because of the abuse she suffered at the hands of her husband. Probably her Psychiatric issues started to manifest during the marriage.

Pam is usually a quiet person but when she gets upset or has a disagreement with a staff member over treatment options, she starts hitting staff.

She had breast cancer which resulted in one of her breasts being removed. When it is time for her chemotherapy she gets upset and wants to fight staff. Pam's chart specifically points out that she is pre-occupied with sex.

# <u>Readmitted</u>

When Dawn was admitted to the Psych Ward a couple of weeks ago, all she talked about was her Daughter getting married. She spoke about how nice her Daughter's future Husband is and she is looking forward to meeting her future Son in Law's family at the wedding.

Dawn's condition was stabilized and she was discharged a couple of days ago. Dawn was so excited that she got discharged in time for her to attend the wedding. But after two weeks Dawn was involuntary readmitted back to the Psych Ward.

Since the day Dawn came back, she was crying; and in between the bouts of crying fits, Dawn expressed what happened that brought her back to the Psych Ward. She said "I was putting out my cigarettes on the wax plate; I thought it was an ashtray. I didn't know it would have melted and made a mess. I only went to my mother's apartment to get something to clean it up. Then my Daughter called the Police. I didn't know…I didn't know…. "

Dawn has been telling everyone who pays her some type of attention that she went over to her elderly Mother's apartment to get something to clean up the mess she made using a wax plate as an ashtray. Yet, it has been documented in her chart that Dawn went over to her Mother's apartment and was arguing with her over money.

The chart stated that Dawn's Daughter called the Police after Dawn became aggressive, belligerent and posed a threat to her elderly Mother. Now she is having some type of psychotic delusion about causing a mess by using a wax plate as an ashtray. It wouldn't surprise the treatment team that Dawn was probably putting out her cigarette on her elderly

Mother. The team definitely knew that Dawn was not taking her medication for a couple of days.

Now it's Sunday, the day of the wedding; now instead of feeling sorry for herself Dawn starts to express anger. She is angry that her Daughter called the Police. She starts ranting how she hates her Daughter; she starts calling her Daughter a conniving and sneaky Jap. She says her Daughter is ungrateful for all the stuff she did for her when she was a girl; and how could she call Police on her own Mother.

Then Dawn started to express that her Mother and Daughter is going to sell her apartment to get rid of her. Once Dawn start to think about the potential sale of her apartment, she begins to cry and express that they are selling the apartment and made plans to keep her locked up in the Psych Ward permanently.

Dawn also verbalize that she would prefer to rot in the streets rather then become a permanent patient in the Psych Ward.

What a wide range of emotions; Dawn paces up and down, feeling sorry for herself, feeling despair, feeling confused, feeling anger, ranting and just talking on and on about her Mother and Daughter; all day, even after her medication was given to her.

It is a wonder that the Psych Ward staff did not sedate her. The behavior only encourages similar type of behaviors among the other Psych Ward patients.

Another patient Katy was also having delusional thoughts and she was also walking around ranting. Sometimes both Dawn and Katy would clash having shouting matches and the only thing that the staff does is to make each one of them go to an opposite side of the ward.  Then they end up shouting at each other again.

Ann Marie was also crying saying that she misses her Mother. Lydia started her delusional ranting and was calling Nurse Shemina who is from India a killer and was telling the Nurse that she is crazy and to keep away from her. Indeed, the Psych Ward was restless.

Well in Dawn's case one needs to put two and two together. Dawn's Daughter did not want Dawn at the wedding. Dawn behaves erratically even after taking her medication. Dawn also has the habit of not taking any medication and it puts herself and the people around her in all types of uncomfortable situations. Why would her Daughter ruin a day that should be one of the happiest moments of her life?

The dilemma for families who has members with mental health issues; if they include them in their lives; there is always some sort or unpredictable turmoil, and instability. Hench, many mentally ill people's families often abandons them or neglects them from being part of family life. They either cannot handle the stress, or do not want the aggravation.

For the families it is time consuming and emotionally draining and the mentally ill person do not appreciate or understand the efforts put in to care for them. The mentally ill can never truly lead an independent life.

# <u>Abandoned</u>

Today was nothing out of the ordinary. A License Clinical Social Worker (LCSW) from the power center came to the Psych Ward to facilitate a group discussion. A few of the patients decided to participate. In this group session the subject of dogs dominated the discussion.

Mike described how he used to own attack dogs, and how those dogs helped him elude police. While two other patients described the type of dogs they used to own. It was a good session; allowing patients to remember a time in their life when something mattered. Being a caretaker of an animal who depended on them for food, shelter; plus, the benefit of having an emotional connection can be a stabilizing factor. This is something that mentally sound people take for granted.

There were other developments in the Psych Ward. Ann-Marie, the young woman from Haiti revealed to the License Clinical Social Worker (LCSW) that she finally contacted her mother and that her mother sent her some money for her birthday.

It is somewhat surprising because according to Ann-Marie's chart, her family abandoned her upon arrival to the United States. They did it by admitting her to the Psych Ward. They never looked back or visited her. Ann-Marie also revealed that her mother used to hit her all the time, but Ann-Marie insists that despite what her mother did to her she still loves her.

This is a typical response of an abused or oppressed person. No matter how they were treated the abuse/oppressed person still look to the abuser/oppressor longing to be accepted. They may actually feel some type of affinity towards the abuser/oppressor.

When it comes to mentally ill people, they tend to get abused by those around them. After all, mentally ill people bring frustration and a lot of stress to those who care for them and the care takers probably have no support in dealing with the mentally ill family member so their frustrations are taken out on the mentally ill person. Then at some point the mentally ill person will eventually be abandoned.

Although in some cases the abandonment may not be intentional. For example, the parents of an autistic child who cannot function on his own may be able to handle the behavior, emotional outburst or even the aggressiveness during the child's younger years. However, when that child and parents becomes older, physically or emotionally the child may become too much for them to handle. So, the hard decision is made to turn the child over to the institutions where there are trained Professionals who are equipped to handle autistic adolescence and adults.

Ann Marie's chart confirms that there was some type of abuse that was meted out by the family because of her slow mental capacity, which climaxed to abuse then physical abandonment, yet Ann-Marie still wants to be connected with her family despite the ill treatment she received from them.

# <u>Crying to Mommy</u>

This week the Psych Ward patients were not as restless as they were last week. One of the developments that took place was that Kevin was readmitted back to the unit on Thursday. Since that time, he has been involved in two altercations with Mike, and he was place on one to one status. This means a staff member will be shadowing him everywhere he goes. Kevin's chart also documented that he instigated the altercation with Mike, and that a female patient reported that he solicited her for sex.

Mike told his Therapist that Kevin started the altercation with him because he got mad when Pam decided to go his room. Mike explained that Kevin wanted to claim ownership over Pam. Despite Kevin's intention of keeping Pam for himself, Pam is pre-occupied with sex and she continues her behavior of entering the rooms of various male patients for the purpose of enticing them to engage in sexual relations.

Mike said that the staff was aware that the fight was over Pam. However, it seems that Mike and Kevin don't get along in general because they had another altercation over a different matter, Kevin continued to rant when he was placed on one to one status. Pam was told to stay away from Kevin.

Pam was also restless, and refused to be weighed. She accused the Nurse on duty of bullying her. During the fresh air period, Pam attacked the Nurse. She was held back by the Aides who escorted her back to the Psych Ward unit.

Dawn looked and sounded more stable then she was last week. However, she has a larger issue looming. According to what Dawn is saying her mother and daughter said that they are going to sell her apartment. She was pre-occupied with this issue, and it was all that she spoke about. She was also cursing her daughter and calling her mother names. At the same time, she was on the phone calling them and pleading them not to sell her apartment; telling them that she would have no place to go.

At one point it seemed that Dawn accepted that the apartment was going to be sold, and asked questions about getting new affordable housing. But most of the time she was pre-occupied with the issue of losing her apartment.

The therapist on duty asked Dawn if she owned a condo, or coop? She said that it was a regular apartment in an apartment building. Then Dawn was asked if she, her mother or daughter owned the apartment building? Dawn stated that they do not own the building. After that Dawn was asked whose name is on the lease? She said her name is on the lease. Then Dawn was told that legally her mother and daughter cannot sell the apartment.

Dawn was also told that by law the owner would have to go to court to get her out of the apartment. At this point the building's owner is not involved in this issue.

In addition, Dawn was also told that the only way her mother and daughter can do anything legally is that they have to have power of attorney over her affairs.

To get the power of attorney they would have to go to court and declare that she is incapable of looking after herself. Dawn stated that her mother and daughter won't be going to court because her mother cannot walk unassisted and her daughter is not going to take time to deal with such matters.

The information that was given to her did little to ease her thoughts. She went to the supervising Nurse and asked whether her mother and daughter could sell her apartment. She received similar information that the therapist had given her. Then she asked the therapist if he can talk to her mother and tell her how she feels. Dawn was told that it would be inappropriate for him to do so. Then she asked the Nurse and was told the same thing.

Mike said he spoke to Dawn's mother during the week at Dawn's request and her mother told him that Dawn acts like a baby and that she spends most of her time in her apartment instead of her own apartment. Mike joked that Dawn's problem is that she has not cut the umbilical cord between her and her mother.

Even though Mike is a patient his metaphor about Dawn's relationship with her mother was spot on. Dawn has an attachment issue towards her mother; and she is constantly calling her and when she was on the outside, she was always spending time at her mother's apartment instead of her own.

Ann-Marie is another patient who has issues with her mother. Even though she admits that her mother used to physically abuse her, and treat her badly. Ann-Marie is always on the phone calling her. The last contact with her mother brought Ann-Marie to tears. So, the Supervising Nurse made comments that Ann-Marie and Dawn are constantly on the phone with their mothers and having emotional reactions after they hang up. So, the Supervising Nurse had the phones turned off. This left both Ann-Marie & Dawn up-set.

Dawn was counseled, and it was explained to her that the phone was turned off to give her a period to cool down. It looked like she accepted what was said, but the pre-occupation of losing her apartment came back and she started crying.

Ann-Marie was also counseled, she was asked if she actually spoke to her mother. She said she actually spoke to her mother. Then she was asked "so why are you crying?" Ann-Marie said she cried because her mother told her that she loved her. Ann-Marie said that when her mother told her that, it made her cry. She said that the Nurse thought that she was crying because she was upset.

Ann-Marie's cry of joy turned into despair because she then started to verbalize that she wants to go home. The Nurse reminded Ann-Marie that she is not in Haiti, or Dominique (Ann-Marie spent time in Psychiatric institutions in France, Haiti and Dominique) and that they cannot let her out just because she wants to leave.

# **<u>Frustration</u>**

There was some frustration between some patients because the phones were off. In response two of the patients Dawn and Jimmy kept on approaching Intern Joseph and pestering him to get the Supervising Nurse to turn the phones on. Intern Joseph said, look the phones are turned off for a reason, and I will not waste my time asking for the phones to be turned on when you know what the answer will be.

Jimmy did not want to accept that the phones are off, he wanted the phones to be turned on and he wanted it to happen now. So, he went to the desk and called out to the Supervising Nurse and accused her of being selfish for not turning on the phones.

Mike saw what Jimmy was doing so he called Jimmy to come over where he was. Mike said, Jimmy stop wasting your time no one will listen to you. Remember they always turn the phones on at lunch time. Sure, enough at the start of lunch, the phones were turned on.

Dawn was in better spirits now that the phones are on and she is able to make the calls she wants to make. She stopped crying about the possibility of her mother and daughter selling her apartment. Dawn said I know they will not sell my apartment; they were only saying it to scare me.

Dawn made an announcement; she said "my daughter and her new husband is coming to visit me." Now that Dawn was at ease about the apartment selling matter and it looks like she made up with her daughter she started being a pest and frustrating  Intern Joseph by constantly asking him to get her things like soda, coffee and cigarettes even though she was repeatedly told that she cannot have those items.

Dawn even asked the intern to lend her some money insisting that she will get the money to repay the loan when her daughter comes to visit; assuring that her daughter will give back the borrowed money.

The frustration carried over to Mike; he was frustrated that he has to hear Dawn ask the same thing over and over again; especially when the staff isn't paying Dawn any mind. Mike shouts to Dawn, "shut the fuck up already!"

Ann-Marie started to cry because she was frustrated that one of the staff members who promised to do her hair was not available to fulfill the promise. The staff member had to be elsewhere to cover for another staff member who called out sick.

Ann- Marie came over to where Mike was and started to cry. This also frustrated Mike; he said she is always doing this; crying when things don't go her way as planned. Jesus Christ! I just feel like slapping the shit out of her!

Now Dawn begins to frustrate the staff because she started to call her mother every ten minutes. She speaks to her mother then calls her back ten minutes later; sometimes the mother picks up but most of the time she doesn't. When she doesn't Dawn gets frustrated. This was the motivating factor for staff to put a limit on all out going phone calls.

When Dawn begins to violate the limitations; staff responded by turning off the phones. Now that the phones are off again, Dawn begins to feel anxious and she verbalizes her frustration.

An altercation begins over the washing machine. Jimmy wanted to use the machine, but Ann-Marie had just put her clothes in the machine. Ann-Marie says Jimmy you can't use the machine now; I just put my clothes in it. Jimmy doesn't listen; he keeps on insisting on using the machine. Ann-Marie gets frustrated and curses him out. Jimmy utters some choice words of his own. The staff tells them to be quiet. Mike starts to show some frustration towards Jimmy.

Apparently, Mike feels that Jimmy is picking on Ann-Marie and arguing with her because she is a female. Mike and Jimmy start to have a war of words. Since Mike has a repetition of having physical altercations this made the staff nervous.

A staff member presses the panic button. Within two minutes four burly men arrived. This calm Mike down somewhat; but Jimmy keeps on mouthing off. One of the Nurses had hopes to stop Jimmy from mouthing off he started to speak with Jimmy in Polish his native language. Mike thinks that the discussion is about him. This frustrates Mike, so he displayed a fit of anger.

The presence of the big men prevents Mike form attacking anyone. One of the Nurses escorts Mike to his room and sedates him with an injection of medication. Then Jimmy was given some medication so that he could be sedated. The Supervising Nurse gave him the choice to take it himself or have it involuntary given.

Now just as things got quite Kevin comes along and started instigating an altercation and talking some smack saying that he is going to body slam somebody. He indirectly insults Dawn by calling her a Prostitute because she gives head in exchange for cigarettes.

He starts to call Ann-Marie Ms. Piggy because of her weight. Dawn heard what Kevin said and starts to mouth off at Kevin. Intern Joseph tells Kevin to stop what he is doing. The Nurse decides that Kevin's thoughts are aggressive and decides to sedate him too.

Dora approached Intern Joseph and told him that she has thoughts of hurting herself. The Intern tells the Supervising Nurse. The Supervising Nurse says, this is Dora's way of seeking attention. So, she calls Dora to the desk and gives her some medication. Later on, the intern checked up on her. Dora says thanks to the medication I feel relaxed.

# **<u>Borderline Personality</u>**

Dora told her Therapist that she hates Joel senior Nurse. She physically shakes at the prospect that he will be on the next shift. Dora said that he used to treat her nice, but he turned on her one day when he was the attending Nurse and placed her on one to one status. She didn't appreciate being shadowed by staff especially the ones she hates.

The senior Nurse was told what Dora revealed. Nurse Joel said that Dora used to like me but since Dora refused to take her medication the staff made the decision to involuntary administer her meds by holding her down and injecting the meds in her. He said Dora thought just because we had a good relationship, that I wouldn't inject her meds in her involuntary. Dora was wrong, and from that time on she looks at me as an enemy.

Today for some apparent reason Dora was very talkative. It was surprising that she approached Intern Joseph to engage in a conversation; this is because she usually won't say anything to anyone unless they are engaging in some type of activity with her.

Dora started telling the Intern about her experiences with some of the staff. She also, started to reminisce about some of her experience during the years that she spent in the Psych Ward. However, she did not want to say how many years she has been in the Psych Ward, perhaps because she holds on to the notion that she will eventually be discharged into her own apartment. Yet she is the one who needs to make the decision to leave. Her treatment team has already expressed that she can leave anytime she wants.

Then Dora started to speak about who she likes and who she doesn't like. A couple of weeks ago Dora told Intern Joseph that she hates one of the Nurses (Neil). Now the Nurse

(Joel) that she hated before, she now likes. The Intern said to Dora, "I thought that you did not like Joel?" Dora did not acknowledge what she said in the past. She just said that he is all right, and pretty cool. The Intern couldn't help but wonder when will he be on Dora's hate list?

Intern Joseph understands that Dora is diagnosed with border line personality disorder. This type of disorder is associated with having intense mood swings, impulsive behavior and extreme reactions. Other symptoms include but not limited to is an unstable self-image or a distorted sense of self, feelings of isolation boredom and emptiness, difficulty feeling empathy for other people, a history of unstable relationships that can change drastically from intense love to intense hate, a persistent fear of abandonment and rejection and intense reaction to abandonment whether being abandoned is real or imaginary; intense highly changeable moods that can last for a few days or hours, impulsive risky behaviors, hostility and unstable career plans and goals. Now the term "border" means that those with this disorder are usually diagnosed with additional mental health disorders such as and not limited to psychosis.

One can see why it is difficult to maintain a relationship with someone who has border line personality disorder. Look at Dora she hates her peers in the Psych Ward and does not want to have anything to do with them. Dora only wants to be associated with staff members, and the little activity that she sometimes engages in it is only with a staff member. However, it seems that the staff does not want to be bothered with Dora. So, you see Dora is surrounded by people but she is a lonely person. That is because she chooses to alienate herself from her peers. However, she has unrealistic expectations of developing a personal relationship with staff members. She does not understand that the staff are professionals who will not compromise the establish ethics of their profession. Well, at least most of them won't.

Sometimes a staff member will play cards, or some other game with her, ask her how she feels and may engage in some small talk with her. But that is in the spirit of fostering good relations and some of the staff genuine care for the patients that they are charged to look after. Other than that, any other type of relationship will violate the Psych Ward standards of conduct and professional ethics.

To compensate Dora engages in attention seeking behavior which includes everything from acting out, having arguments with other Psych Ward Patients to attempting suicide and even faking suicide attempts.

Dora who really needs to be in an assisted living facility in the outside world is lingering and wasting away being locked up in the Psych Ward because she does not want to leave. She refuses to engage in therapy other than taking medication. She makes no plans for her future other than contemplating what behavior she will do to get attention from staff.

# <u>Mike the Blood</u>

Interns Joe often sits down and has informal talks with the patients in the Psych ward. Joe has a personal interest in getting to know each patient outside of what is written in their charts. This way the patients may develop the feelings that Joe generally cares about their welfare and is more liable to open up and express themselves during a group or individual counseling session; or if anything is on their mind, their thoughts, ideas and even their life's philosophy. Yes, it is hard to believe that mentally ill people who have schizophrenia, unrealistic and psychotic delusions have any philosophy concept. Yet many of them do.

One needs to understand that some mental illness is a development, it may come to some early in life, for others it comes later in life, or as a result of head trauma, or an unpleasant experienced; whether that experience is real or imagined. The medical community has not pin pointed the causes but there are lots of theories out there which actually holds water if one should study it.

Mike is one of the colorful characters in the Psych ward. Mike opened up to Joe and started to tell him his personal experience. Mike's personal experience is kind of interesting. Mike has been in and out of various Psych wards since childhood. Mike's mental illness developed early in life. You may say that it developed before his life started. During his time in the womb Mike's mother was abusing drugs. Whatever drug she took was passed onto Mike. Ultimately Mike was born addicted to crack. By the time Mike was in Kindergarten he was first diagnosed as being semi-retarded and was already spending time in a Psych Ward.

According to Mike it seems his mother cleaned up some because he said out of all the children in the Psych Ward he was the only one whose mother made regular visits; Mike said my "mother used to visit me every day and when she came she used to bring presents for the other children and play with them; she felt sorry that their mothers never came to see them. The other kids even called my mother mama."

By the time Mike reached his teenage years he was stable enough to live outside the Psych ward, but unfortunately his mother passed away. He went to live with his Aunt down south. The Aunt and her Husband owned a restaurant and Mike and his Cousins worked in the restaurant.

During his early twenties Mike returned to the city and started living a life of hustling. He started working for a drug dealer selling drugs and running errands for the dealer. Mike said "the dealer used to walk around with a gun, beat people up and threaten to kill them." "He used to give me the gun and send me and a couple of guys to go collect money from people that owed him. One day I got into an argument with someone, I was so mad I was wanted to kill him. I went to the dealer to get the gun; but the dealer refused to give it to me. The dealer told everyone else not to give me anything. The fucking dealer talked all that shit about killing, but refused to give me the gun when I wanted to kill someone." What mike doesn't realize is that the drug dealer had a conscious and did Mike a favor by not giving him the gun when he felt like killing someone.

Mike did not elaborate on how many times he got arrested. But since his mental capacity is impaired, he fell in the category of not being charged or convicted because of being mentally unfit to stand trial.

He becomes part of the vicious cycle of being held in the lock up for a couple of days after being arrested, brought before a judge who rules he is mentally unfit for trial, then spends a couple of more days or weeks in the lock up then on court order shipped to the Psych Ward where he will spend a couple of months before being released back into the community. When he commits the next crime the cycle repeats.

But in a strange twist of fate, there are consequences for patients in the Psych Ward if they commit crimes against staff? Psych Ward staff face the possibility of being assaulted. This is an occupational hazard of working with the mentally unfit.

Assaults come in the form of gestures, verbal, physical or sexual. Mike recently returned back to the Psych Ward after spending a couple of months on Rikers Island after being charged with sexually assaulting a female staff member.

As it stands the lock up have its own culture. Mike revealed that he became a member of the BLOOD nation. Mike says the motto is MOB (Money Over Bitches). Mike goes to his room and brings out a legal pad. Mike says, I'm not supposed to show anyone this, it would get me killed. They wrote it down for me so that I can remember it. Mike takes a cocktail of medication which compromises his short-term recall abilities. What was written revealed some information about the BLOOD nation.

BLOOD is an acronym for Brotherly Love Overrides Oppression & Destruction.

There was a picture of the Star of David with a number 5.

The BLOODS have their own coded language. It is numbers and phases that relates to certain terms and actions. The codes are updated and frequently changed. There were symbols written down that they wanted Mike to remember:

True George

MOB= Money over bitches

009 = what's up

012 = Looking

013 = Tear him up

015= Let me know get back to me

025 = You sure

031= blood love

038 = Hold On

044 = Blood, it ain't easy but it sure is fun

050 = stay on point

067 = Ghetto Star

069 = Shake down

SMM= sex money murder

OG=Original gangster.

K-9 = Police

123-You're in Violation

There are other numerous acronyms and symbols that have meaning to members of the BLOOD. Mike didn't have them all written down only the ones that was important for him to remember in the Riker's Island environment.

Mike also mentions about the different types of hand gestures. To Intern Joe, it surely looks like this gang stuff emulates the secret societies who have coded hand gestures, coded language, symbols, signs, culture, even rites and rituals just like the Masons. If one should think about it; its exactly the same. Isn't it strange how a society breeds its own monsters?

# **<u>Race Card</u>**

A new Intern was assigned to the Psych Ward so now there are two Interns who will be on site on the same days and time. The first Intern wonders how things will work out since whatever activity that takes place in the Psych Ward is initiated and run by him.

The staff is supposed to help, but the staff doesn't help, they don't want to be bothered with the patients outside of their official functions. You can't really blame the staff for having this type of attitude after all dealing with mentally ill people is a drain on one's energy. Plus, if the staff member does not have some measure of patience and are not prepared to have a physical confrontation with patients who are having a psychotic breakdown, or cannot control their emotions; then being in the mental health field would not be for them.

Now that the new Intern has started, it was interested so see how the patients behave since this Intern began. The new Intern (Gary) is a white male as oppose to the first Intern (Joseph) who is black. The first intern could not establish rapport or some sort of relationship with the majority of white male patients; they do not participate in groups or card games with him.

Before Joseph came along the Intern whom he replaced was a white Female. She had a better success rate among the white female, blacks (male & female), Jewish (male & female) and Muslim patients. It is ironic that there are virtually no Muslim female patients in the psych ward. Now that Intern Gary is on site, the white male patients approach him and engage in conversation and individual counseling and groups activity.

One of the reasons for this is that the Psych ward is like a prison. The exception is that the Psych ward does not have bars on the windows and the staff are not correction officers. At least 85 % of the Psych Ward patients have spent some time in prison.

When they are admitted to the Psych ward, they bring the prison mentality and culture with them. When they mingle with their fellow patients, they often pick who they associate with by race. If it isn't by race then it is by religion.

For example, the white patients will befriend other white patients before they befriend nonwhites; black patients will befriend other black patients before that will befriend patients outside their race.

When it comes to religion race doesn't matter. The Jewish patients will befriend another Jewish patient before they befriend a non-Jewish patient; The same goes for Muslims and Christians. For the female patients race or religion is not a factor.

All is not lost because the two Interns have a mutual understanding to work as a team. Now when there is group activity it is a joint effort combining the participating patients into one group session.

Those who did not participate in group sessions before because they did not like the racial makeup of the group or the group leader are now participating making the group sessions racial make up more diverse.

Now that the new Intern Gary started doing his internship hours; Richard the youngest white patient was open to sitting down with him to discuss what is on his mind.

Richard has never sat down and spoke for a length of time with anyone.    Denny an older white male patient in the unit also sat down and spoke with Intern Gary. It was observed that there was a group discussion among the white males at one point. Before Intern Gary the white males have never voluntary participated in any group discussion. This has reinforced that there is some type of identification with the race of the counselor as far as male patients are concerned.

Meanwhile it is recognized that there has been some progress with the first Intern, Joseph in gaining rapport with some patients who did not speak with him before. The first one is Bryan he is another young white male; however, he is withdrawn and keeps to himself. Bryan just happened to sit at the table where Intern Joseph was sitting to eat lunch.

Intern Joseph decided to see if he would respond if he asked him a question. Intern Joseph asked Bryan something like "what do you like to do?" Bryan answered, "I like to draw;" Intern Joe then asked "what kind of picture would you like to draw?" Bryan's responded "I like to draw words," It seems that Bryan likes to draw words instead of drawing pictures.

The other person who has never spoken to Joe before is Richard. It was surprising that Richard actually sat down with Intern Joseph and engaged in the group activity of playing a card game. Even though it was for a brief moment, Intern Joseph welcomed it.

Intern Joe was told by two staff members how they feel about his participation in the Psych Ward. Staff member Sade stated that Intern Joseph have developed some form of trust among the black patients. Since most of the staff and patients are white the black patients felt some type of mistrust or racial tension. Intern Joseph's presence made some of the black patients feel more comfortable.

Another staff member James has also given Intern Joseph a compliment and said that since Intern Joe came to the unit there has been an increase in activity among some of the patients. Intern Joseph's time with the Psych Ward will be over soon and he hopes that whoever does his evaluation feels the same way.

Overall, it seems that the small gesture in attempting to gain rapport with the goal to have a discussion is having some effect. However, the Interns still have to remember that the patients are medicated and that the medication has a huge impact on how they feel, whether or not to engage in some form of activity; or just sit down and have a discussion.

# **<u>Violations</u>**

It was business as usual in the Psych Ward; nothing out of the ordinary took place. The only thing that tried the patience of Intern Joseph was Dawn. She keeps on asking him if he can go to the cafeteria and buy her some coffee. She tells the Intern Joseph that she has money and will pay him $10 if he can go and get her a cup of coffee. Other times she would pester him if he can sell her a cigarette.

Intern Joseph keeps on telling Dawn the same answer over and over and over again. Intern Joseph states that "I cannot do these things for you." Dawn was persistent and Intern Joseph was standing his ground.

It got to the point where one of the other patients mentioned that she is just wasting her time asking for something that she will not receive.

Gary the other Intern mentioned that Dawn is the only patient that he felt some type of discomfort when she approaches him. Intern Gary avoids interacting with Dawn whenever he can.

The reason why Dawn is harassing the Interns is that she cannot get to go to the cafeteria to get what she wants because she has committed some type of violation of the Psych ward rules, since the Interns are not always there; she thought that they would go out their way to do something for her that the regular staff would not do.

When someone comes to visit a patient, there are rules in place that is designed to keep the patients as well as the visitors safe. Yet, some of the patient's visitors violate the unit rules on providing certain things that can be dangerous to the patients.

The anorexia patient Lydia's visitor who is her sister was told not to give Lydia any more gum. This is because Lydia has a habit of putting the whole pack of gum in her mouth and going to sleep. When she goes to bed and sleeps with chewing gum in her mouth the gum winds up being stuck in her throat. The last time this happened, she almost died.

The Psych Ward administration has forbidden Lydia from chewing gum. But Lydia's sister has given in to Lydia's begging and brought her some gum during her visitation. Lydia was so happy to finally have some chewing gum again after a lengthy time period.

Unfortunately for Lydia the staff is more attentive when it comes to her because she is just as physically fragile as she is mentally. They noticed that she was chewing gum. The staff forced her to spit out the gum and her body, room and belongings were searched to make sure that she doesn't have any more gum.

The other visitor violations were that Kevin's visitor provided Kevin with cigarettes. Then Kevin and Richard hid in the bathroom and were smoking. They wouldn't have gotten caught if it wasn't for Richard asking to go out for some fresh air after the fresh air group already left. The staff smelled the smoke on him. When the staff confronted them about the smoking; both Kevin and Richard confessed to having the cigarettes and they even told who provided it to them.

Whether or not the visitors intentional violated the Psych Ward rules the staff is required to report what took place to the treatment team. The treatment team will then make the decision whether to ban the visitors who violated the rules from visiting for a periiod of time. The treatment team can also decide to take away a patient's privileges.

If patient privileges were to be taken away; the patients would no longer be able to walk the grounds, or go to the cafeteria by themselves during the week.

In the case of Lydia, she is deemed a high risk and cannot go anyplace anyway (not that she cares). Lydia won't even care if her sister doesn't visit. She is always expressing that she hates her sister. On the other hand, Kevin and Richard won't be happy campers if they are sanctioned in any way.

# <u>Accusations</u>

Pam was having a psychotic episode; she was verbalizing that she was raped. Whether there is some validity to this claim is a mystery. The staff isn't paying Pamela any attention as far as her claim of being raped is concerned.

The problem is that Pamela is pre-occupied with sex and she solicits sex from all of the male patients. She goes as far as to sneak into the male patient's room for the purpose of having sex.

Sometimes she engages in sexual activity with more than one male at the same time. Another reason; one of Pamela's disorders is being a psychotic; and whatever psychotic delusion she may have does not have to be based on reality, or a past experience.

Between the psychotic rants of being a rape victim she is usually reserved and does not interact with anyone. But this weekend she sat down and actually participated in a group function and played a hand of cards with other patients. After the card game during visiting hours Pamela started ranting about being rapped again.

When her parents came to visit, she became agitated; and when the psychotic delusions hit; she started to openly accuse her father of raping her. The more she accused her father of rape; the more aggressive she got. Things were escalating so much that two staff members intervened.

Staff intervention did little to de-escalate the situation. It only made Pam become more aggressive that she started to lash out at the staff members and hit them. When Pam's mother attempted to calm her down Pam slapped her. So now that Pamela was out of control a staff member pressed the panic button; and the three big burly men came into the unit and restrained Pam. While the big guys were restraining her the nurse on duty gave Pamela a shot and she was sedated. Hopefully she should be calm when she wakes up.

# **<u>Christopher's Faith</u>**

Chris asked Intern Joseph if he could get some literature on Islam. He said that Mike was encouraging him to speak on some black history in the auditorium when black history month arrives. Chris decided that he wants to speak about Islam.

At the request of Chris, the Intern Joseph got some literature on Elijah Muhammad. The Intern figured that if he brought in the information on Elijah Muhammad, he can engage Chris in some sort of discussion.

Chris is one of the few patients in the Psych Ward that will sit down and discuss some sort of topic. But due to Chris's mental capacity, he cannot focus on one topic for long; he jumps from one subject to the next subject. Yet, the discussion on Elijah Muhammad went well and time pasted quickly.

Another benefit that came out of the discussion was that Chris started to open up more to Intern Joseph; he started to reveal some aspect of his own life experience. This was a good development because Chris normally does not talk about his past.

Of all the things that Chris mentioned the one thing that he expressed congruently of his life's experience was that him and his brother were adopted, and that the family who adopted him was Muslim. However, because of Chris's mental condition he was not focused on any one period of his life; he was jumping from one period to another with gaps between them. At one point, he asked Intern Joseph when he converted to Islam.

Intern Joseph told him that he is not a Muslim; and that what he knows about Islam is based on the material that he researches as well as speaking with a friend who happens to be an Iman. Then Chris asked why do you carry the Quran around?  Intern Joseph explained, "I also read the Torah and Bible and have electronic copies of them on my phone." Chris said I thought you were Muslim because of your beard. The intern said, "Now Chris, please understand that there are common aspects to Islam, Christianity and Judaism and that having a beard is one of them."

All of a sudden Chris started to shift his focus which he often does; if you do not pay attention to what he is talking about, whatever he utters may sound gibberish and you'll be lost as to what he is expressing. Now Chris went from talking about his life to talking about the situation that happened recently with Mike.

Chris felt that it was his fault that Mike became aggressive, and he felt guilty when the staff held Mike down, gave him an injection and took him away. Intern Joseph asked "how is it that you feel it is your fault?"  Chris stated that before the incident him and Mike were engaging in a Salah (Arabic for prayer).  Chris stated that he thought he felt a connection with Mike while they prayed together. Then shortly after they finished preying, the incident with Mike and the staff took place.

Intern Joseph assured Chris that what took place with Mike was not his fault and that Mike has a history of behaving the way he behaves, and that Mike has many things going on in his mind that has nothing to do with engaging in the Salah.

Chris gave some insight to the incident; it seemed that Mike had some built-up resentment towards one of the Doctors.

Chris revealed that Mike discussed it with him on one occasion. However, the Intern attempted to make Chris become aware that the only person that can fully explain Mike's actions is Mike.

Intern Joseph managed to get Chris to semi focus on his plans of speaking about Islam during the Psych Ward's Black History Month festivities. To the Intern Joseph's dismay, Chris has not demonstrated that he is capable to understand or even summarize the material that was presented to him it is just too complex for Chris's fragile mental state.

It was a learning experience for Intern Joseph; he realized that Chris had an unrealistic goal. His mental condition does not allow him to have the capacity make a speech on any topic.

When Chris first spoke about making a public speech in front of other people the Intern didn't get that Chris was being delusional; now the Intern understands that a delusional person cannot tell the difference between imagination and reality.

# **<u>Expressions</u>**

The Psych Ward is being reorganized and the expansion phase has taken effect. The Psych Ward now occupies an entire floor in the Hospital complex. It has been renamed Psych Ward East and Psych Ward West. Psych Ward West is the expansion unit. Both Psych Ward East and Psych Ward West will be headed by the same clinical Director and Treatment Team Leader.

Some of the patients that are in Psych Ward East have been moved to Psych Ward West. The patients that are still left in Psych Ward East are the patients with the more colorful personalities. They are the ones who stand out and exhibit expressive behaviors that medication cannot control or suppress.

Most of the time the expressive behavior is not violent; it gives a unique perspective among the patients who otherwise remain silent and do not express themselves as long as they are medicated.

One example is Dora. She is diagnosed as being borderline personality she does not like her fellow patients; she hates some more than others. She hates some staff members and recently she flips flopped on Intern Gary.

When Intern Gary first came aboard, she took a liking to him. Now she hates him. Intern Joseph wonders what is his status with Dora? Dora still interacts with Intern Joseph which tells him that he isn't on her hate list.

As a bonus to Intern Joseph she usually reveals the latest events that take place in the Psych Ward; at least Intern Joseph gets to know what's happening from a patient's perspective.

Earlier Dora caused a ruckus because she did not want another patient that she hates sitting next to her. It was during snack time; Dawn sat at her table because all the other tables were taken. Dora objected that Dawn sat next to her but the staff told Dora that Dawn has every right so sit where she wants too. Dora took offense and screamed at the top of her lungs; then she took Dawn's juice and threw it on the floor.

Another patient who often expresses herself in ways that medication cannot control or suppress is Kate. She also caused a ruckus; the expressive behavior that Kate exhibits is to verbalize her thoughts and feelings in a loud voice.

If someone says something to her about her verbal expressions, she raises her voice even louder. However, this time around Kate had a legitimate concern that she verbalized; but her delusional perspective prevailed over the legitimate complaint.

Kate has the delusional idea that some members of her family were murdered. If you didn't know Kate what she says about the murder of members of her family sounds convincing. It's so convincing that if she would report it to the Police; they will open up an investigation.

Kate is a long-term patient and she is so delusional that whatever she says about her past cannot be believed. However, her chart that contains her documented personal history states that there is no evidence that members of her family were murdered.

The spin on this psychotic belief that members of her family were murdered is that she said that the perpetrator of the murders is Kevin. Kate is fixated on Kevin; she also started to verbalized that Kevin is not a good person and blames him for things that have nothing to do him.

It is interesting how Kevin's repetition precedes itself. Everyone in the Psych Ward, from management, to staff, to patients say that Kevin is a shady person and cannot be trusted.

Even patients and staff, who have spoken to Kevin for the first time, concluded that Kevin's character is shady; yet, Kevin's chart reveals that he is not a criminal; he never spent time on Rikers Island or the state penitentiary like some of his fellow patients have.

His chart also reveals that he is promiscuous and that he has commitment issues and just cannot be trusted to follow through with anything. Kevin is perceived as being a con artist. When he plays a game with his fellow patients, he walks away from the game if he is losing.

The last group interaction with Kevin was less then positive. The problem was when he began to say negative verbal remarks that made his card playing partner feel bad.

His partner Nadia has a fragile mental state. She is prone to depression, the reason she is in the Psych Ward is because she attempted to commit suicide and Kevin's berating would have led her back into a depressed mood; all because Kevin did not like the fact, they were losing a card game.

Intern Joseph had to step in and told Kevin to stop the verbal abuse and if he wants to continue playing the game with the group, he has to treat his partner with respect. Kevin's reaction was to stand up and walk away like he usually does; but this time he came back later and apologized.

Lydia, the anorexic patient made her usual objections to taking the weight maintainer nutritional substance; and as usually she started to cry. However, it is recognized that her behavior of crying is nothing but crocodile tears. She rants accusing staff of trying to kill her and it is usually followed up by her crying act.

Observing the expressive behaviors is comical and would make you laugh.  If someone who does not know that the individuals in the Psych Ward are mentally ill, they would get the perception that the delusional accusations are legitimate rather than a case of psychosis.  But what is not a laughing a matter is that the delusional expressive behaviors are real to the patients and the patients would either hurt themselves or others over it.

# **<u>Dora's Incident</u>**

The Intern Joseph was called in by the supervising Nurse Marge, she wanted to give the Intern the experience to counsel two people; one was a patient who recently attempted to commit suicide and the other was the attending Nurse who was on duty when the incident happened.

The Nurse Ron is an immigrant from Poland who have been living and working in the City for a couple of years; he told Intern Joseph that Dora attempted to commit suicide during lunch.

She stuffed bread down her throat; yet, somehow, she alerted the staff that she was choking. Nurse Ron said by the time I got to her she was unconscious. I was very lucky to resuscitate her before brain damaged set in.  Man, when I used to work in a senior care home I used to see when they died. I expected them to die because of their advance age. But I have never dealt with someone who attempted suicide. This has shaken me up, and I believe the other patients are traumatized because of Dora's actions.

Intern Joseph tells Ron, it is good that you are talking about how you felt when the incident happened. I think that you are also traumatized, perhaps you should see the folks in the Employee Assistance Program (EAP), and they will help you to sort out your feelings. But be aware that incidents like this are going to happen in here once in a while.

Intern Joe went over to Dora to find out how she was feeling when she decided her suicide attempt. Dora is a long-time patient in the unit. Dora was diagnosed as a borderline personality. Dora was also diagnosed with social anxiety disorder.  Dora likes to be the center of attention and does things to seek attention; however, she does not like her fellow patients and she rarely interacts and speaks with them. She has been a patient in the psych ward for the past five years.

The unique thing about Dora is that she doesn't have to be in the psych ward. Right now, she is there by choice. She was told that the Psychologist said that she does not belong in the unit and that she could live among people outside the psych ward.

He recommended that she be transitioned into an assisted living home. However, Dora refuses to leave the psych ward, yet the hospital isn't putting pressure on her to leave. So, to speak, Dora self-imposed herself to the restrictive environment of the psych ward.

Dora has a history of attempted suicide and she also faked suicide attempts to get people to pay her some attention. Intern Joseph sat down with Dora and asked her about the incident. Dora said; I did not attempt to commit suicide. All I can remember is that I was eating then the next thing I know; I was on the floor and the staff was on top of me. They told me that I lost conscience.

Dora refused to acknowledge that she attempted to commit suicide. Yet, the attending caseworker that was present when the incident took place immediately spoke with Dora, and Dora admitted that she made a suicide attempt.

She admitted she stuffed the bread down her throat to choke herself; however, when she felt the pain of not being able to breathe; she got scared and alerted staff. Now, she is telling Intern Joseph that she did not attempt to commit suicide.

The only consolation that happened was that Dora wrote a note to Intern Joe. The note stated "I'm depressed, I'm confused and I don't want to hurt myself."

Perhaps Dora needs to be in the psych ward after all; she won't get the attention she gets living among everyday people. Most people would not put up with her antics and she will emotional drain those around her.

# <u>Leaving</u>

In the Psych Ward it was business as usual; however, Pedro a patient that usually initiates some type of activity such as card playing or board games among his peers is no longer in the unit. Pedro was the type of patient that will develop a quick rapport with newly assigned staff. Yet, for the past couple of weeks he was supposed to be discharged. The problem is that Pedro wouldn't agree with any of the discharged conditions.

First Pedro was told to make an appointment with a Doctor which he refused to do. Then Pedro was told that he had to apply for social security benefits; he refused to do it. Pedro was also told that as a condition of discharged he must have some type of housing arrangement. Pedro made no move to secure any type of housing.

Whatever attempts that the Psych Ward administration did to help Pedro find housing Pedro disagreed with the type of housing that was found. Now Pedro is complaining that he feels that he has been in the inpatient unit too long (2 years) and that people who had worse mental health symptoms then has was discharged sooner.

It's too bad for Pedro that he does not recognize that he is still in the inpatient because of his mental health condition. Pedro does not want to do anything that will allow the Psych Ward to discharge him. Pedro also does not recognize that those who have what he perceived to be a worse mental health symptom was discharged because they have fulfilled the requirements that is necessary for the Psych Ward to discharge them.

Now despite that Pedro does not want to agree to apply for social security, public assistance, or secure housing; he had found a way to get out of the Psych Ward. It may not have been through official channels, and I'm sure that nobody will recommend what Pedro did to leave the Psych Ward to other Psych Ward patients. You see Pedro took advantage of the system and took a loop hole out.

What happened was that Pedro had a court date concerning the charges that landed him in the Psych Ward. The courts were checking to see if he is still not mentally fit to answer to the criminal charges before dismissing the case. Pedro's Public Defender made the case and lucky for Pedro the charges were dismissed.

After Pedro left the court room and while he was waiting in the court house hallways for the Psych Ward staff member to come and escort him back to the Psych Ward. Pedro decided to blend in with a group of people heading to the elevator. Pedro huddled with the crowd and made it down to the lobby and he went out the court house doors. Now Pedro is no longer an inpatient at the Psych Ward. Instead Pedro is now a Psychiatric fugitive.

Pedro's escape was reported to the Police; but there will be no active man hunt. The Police and Psych Ward officials know that it will be a be a matter of time before Pedro will do something to get himself arrested and shipped back to the Psych Ward.